Freedom and Circumstance: Philosophy in Ortega y Gasset

by Oswald Sobrino

Copyright © 2011 Oswald Sobrino
All rights reserved.

To Maria Teresa

Whose question on the streets of Madrid sparked this overdue book

TABLE OF CONTENTS

INTRODUCTION 5

CHAPTER 1   FIRST, WHO WAS ORTEGA? 9

CHAPTER 2   SURPASSING MODERN PHILOSOPHY 14

CHAPTER 3   CHRISTIANITY AND THE DISCOVERY
OF SUBJECTIVITY 20

CHAPTER 4   STARTING AGAIN 24

CHAPTER 5   WHAT IS LIVING? 32

CONCLUSION: WHAT THEN IS PHILOSOPHY? 36

Author Oswald Sobrino 38

Suggested Reading and Bibliography 39

NOTES 41

INTRODUCTION

Many in the English-speaking world have studied philosophy in college and have never heard of the Spanish philosopher José Ortega y Gasset (1883-1955). That fact, in my view, reflects the blinders that we wear in the English-speaking world. We tend to think in terms of the British Isles first and then France and Germany when it comes to most intellectual matters, especially in the humanities. Whether we wish to admit it or not, the Hispanic cultural world is often viewed as, at best, a distant poor cousin. In the Hispanic cultural world, Ortega's place is secure. His genius alone should secure his place in our contemporary English-speaking world.[1]

This book will introduce you to Ortega not as a way to provide a politically correct dosage of diversity to my fellow English-speakers but first and foremost to introduce a philosophical writer, eloquent and gifted even in translation, whose insights will, I believe, stir your soul because his incisive insights resonate so much with our personal lived experience.

One of the great interpreters and students of Ortega was the philosopher and prolific writer Julián Marías (1914-2005), who was a personal friend, student, and colleague of Ortega and who survived Ortega by half a century. Marías wrote prolifically; but his best known work is his *History of Philosophy,* a best seller in the Spanish-speaking world and, thankfully, published in English translation by Dover Books. Marías' *History* is itself a little masterpiece of orderly clarity in recounting the history of Western philosophy. It has even been used on the undergraduate philosophy level at the American Catholic seminary where I teach as an adjunct professor. (You can find my author information after the "Conclusion.")

Marías was also not lacking in *chutzpah*. He closes his *History* with a treatment of Ortega's philosophy and pulls no punches in proudly stating, in a way that always brings a wry smile to my lips, that:

> We have followed the entire history of Western philosophy century by century and stage by stage, from Greece to Ortega and the philosophical group originated by him. God has allowed us to close this history, as is just, with Spanish names.[2]

What exactly did he mean by this apparent boast? I am reminded of what Jesus says in the Gospels when he thanks the Father for revealing wisdom to the simple rather than to the wise and learned (see Matthew 11:25). Well, both Ortega and Marías were quite learned and even erudite. Yet Spain herself was for a very long time a philosophical backwater since her glory days in late antiquity and in the Middle Ages with great Christian, Jewish, and Muslim thinkers such as Isidore of Seville, Averroës, and Maimonides, and since the era of the great Thomistic philosopher Francisco Suárez (1548-1617), known as the "Excellent Doctor" (*Doctor Eximius*). Even earlier, the great Stoic Seneca and even the Stoic emperor Marcus Aurelius emerged from the Hispano-

Roman world. So, maybe, in Marías eyes, it was "just" that philosophy finally came *back* into her own in Spain with the work of Ortega in the twentieth century. There is a lesson here for other nations and individuals looking to restore lost intellectual greatness and vigor. Renewal is possible.

In the end, you will be the judge of whether Ortega's insights are truly of world significance. My job is to invite you to make that assessment for yourself. I will make that invitation by drawing attention to some of Ortega's insights in a work that arose from lectures he gave to students and the general public in Madrid in 1929 (the fact that the venue of the lectures ended up being a theatre tells you something about his own speaking abilities and about his public stature). The fundamental nature of the title of this lecture series--*What is Philosophy?*-- indicates why I chose this work out of so many other Orteguian works (and possibly the first in a series of books by me on Ortega's writings). This book will let Ortega answer that question for you, a question that is, from the Orteguian point of view, vital for your life and mine because as humans we have an urgent and dramatic need to philosophize in the circumstances of our lives. Test these insights against your own experience of life. In the end, you are the ultimate judge, as long as you purposefully decide to listen with an open mind and to put aside any unjustified cultural prejudices and low expectations. The wise person keeps an open mind and is able to suspend premature judgment; otherwise, he forecloses learning.

Although there is a fine English translation of Ortega's *What is Philosophy?*[3] (*¿Qué es filosofía?*), I will provide in this book my own translations from the Spanish text contained in the collection of Ortega's works edited by the scholar Paulino Garagorri.[4] If you wish to compare my translations to the original Spanish, that is the place to go; and I urge any with the skills to do so to savor Ortega's forceful and incisive Spanish style for themselves. It has been tempting at several points in writing this short book (whose brevity I consider a virtue in a world of books that are verbose) to simply translate Ortega for you since his prose is masterful. Thus, I must urge you to read his works directly in Spanish or in English translation to truly taste what makes Ortega so appealing to many of us. And so, let us start the journey. ¡*Vamos*!

CHAPTER 1 FIRST, WHO WAS ORTEGA?

He was born and died in Madrid. If geography is destiny, as Napoleon is supposed to have remarked, then Ortega's having been born, having matured, and having died in Madrid, put Ortega in the very geographic and political heart of Spain and on the edge of Europe, both physically and culturally. As we will see, Ortega's philosophy emphasized one's particular circumstances, the precise circumstances that give rise to one's individual perspective on reality. For Ortega, the Spanish reality with all of its glories and admitted and obvious frustrations, with its joys and its depressing aspects, would color his whole life. His personal mission was to bring Spain up to, in his phrase, "the height of the times." As his most loyal disciple Marías noted, "throughout his entire life" Ortega "was to subordinate every other present circumstance to the Spanish one."[5]

Yet, that Spanish focus never made Ortega a parochial man. He was always the universal man, the intellectual who easily quoted and referred to a Latin, Greek, German, or Italian saying or even to the culture of the Far East. In fact, his personal preoccupation with elevating Spain to the "height of the times" made him an emphatic European with a Europeanism that foreshadowed the effort to build a united Europe after the disastrous Second World War. In these times of economic turmoil in the European Union, it may be useful on another occasion to return to this aspect of Ortega's life-project.

In addition, to grappling with the challenges of Spanish backwardness, Ortega embraced a personal mission to make philosophy a topic of interest to the broader reading public of Spain and also to the reading public of the rest of the Spanish-speaking world. I can personally testify to his success in doing so in the wider Hispanic world. My own Cuban father—who never attended a university—read and collected Ortega's books. My strong suspicion is that this appeal to those outside the university extended to many others like my father in the Spanish-speaking world.

Yet, to remedy the Spanish situation, Ortega himself first had to become a philosopher on the cutting edge of European philosophy. To meet this requirement, he travelled to Germany to study philosophy and related subjects between 1905 and 1911, with financial support from the Spanish government.[6] Thus, to remedy a very particular national situation required Ortega to become the opposite of the parochial or inward-looking native who does not care to look beyond his village, beyond the shire. *To really understand the particular and to reform it requires looking well beyond the particular.* That intellectual requirement is why Ortega cannot be dismissed as merely a philosopher for Spain or the Spanish-speaking. He is a philosopher for all who face the urgent need to transform their circumstances wherever those particular circumstances are found. Many of us are in that category. All of us should be.

After receiving his doctorate in 1904, Ortega became professor of metaphysics (the branch of philosophy concerned with the structure of being itself) at the University of Madrid, a post which he held until the massive disruption of the Spanish Civil War in 1936, which led to his temporary exile from Spain until the nineteen forties.[7] During his intellectual career, Ortega did not remain in an ivory tower. He wrote widely in newspapers, appropriately so for someone born into a family of journalists. Yet, the writing in newspapers, along with his custom of public lecturing outside the classroom, was not a mere quirk. Ortega wanted to take philosophy "into the street" as part of his personal mission to rejuvenate his beloved and frustrating Spain. I have no doubt that today Ortega would be a blogger amazed at the reach and speed of today's technology and its potential for reaching a wide and international public. The serialized newspaper article was the closest thing to a blog that he had at his disposal. He was essentially a man on a "mission," a concept which, as we shall see, plays a significant role in his philosophy of human life.

In the nineteen fifties, as his life was nearing its end, Ortega spoke outside of Spain in other parts of Europe and even in the United States. The German University of Marburg, where he had cut his teeth in Neo-Kantian philosophy so many decades earlier, granted him an honorary doctorate.[8] It should also be noted that Ortega's theoretical achievements are comparable, if not superior, to those of the celebrated German philosopher Heidegger, who knew Ortega personally.[9] That comparison is important because some consider Heidegger to be the greatest philosopher of the twentieth century.

Today, in Madrid and Toledo, Spain, the José Ortega y Gasset Foundation, with branches in Latin America, continues his intellectual and educational mission and publishes, among other journals, the famous *Revista de Occidente* ("Journal of the West") founded by Ortega in 1923.[10] Spain's highest award for journalistic achievement is called the José Ortega y Gasset Prize.[11] All in all, Ortega lived a full life as an engaged intellectual and man of letters, engaged in a profound educational mission until his death and engaged even in politics during the Spanish Republic of the nineteen thirties. To borrow from the vocabulary of Ortega's philosophy, he transformed and "reabsorbed" his particular circumstances; and we still see the effects today. His philosophical legacy is too important to be simply a matter of interest for the Spanish-speaking world (although, today, that world is again crucially important for the entire globe and even includes the United States as the second-largest Spanish-speaking nation on the planet). This book aims to bring that philosophical legacy to more English-speakers because the philosophical insights are too vitally important to ignore.

Finally, another important point to emphasize in any introduction of Ortega concerns his method of presentation. He makes a marvelous comparison in describing his own method of philosophizing: "Great philosophical problems require the use of a tactic similar to that used by the Hebrews to capture Jericho and its secret places: without a direct attack, circling around it slowly, narrowing their path further with each lap and loudly keeping up in the air the sound of their dramatic trumpets."[12] Those familiar with the writings of the late John Paul II will recognize this same "spiralling" method of approaching a challenging intellectual problem, whether philosophical or theological. Maybe, that similarity is no accident, given that both men were philosophers very much influenced by the phenomenological tradition.

What this self-conscious "Jericho" method of conquering a problem tells us is that we should be patient in reading Ortega—he will eventually tie all of the loose ends together. In fact, Ortega himself notes how prosaic and simple his terms appear at first blush, only to eventually acquire a more rigorous, theoretical content.[13] I submit that this method is very much what attracted so many students to Ortega's lectures. As his students noted, attending the lectures of Ortega was to experience and watch the very act and process of philosophizing taking place before one's very eyes.[14] Ortega invites us to witness and join in the act of philosophizing as a vital necessity.

This recollection by one of his students captures Ortega while philosophizing in the lecture hall:

It is nine o'clock in the morning; the lecture room, with a window overlooking the garden of the Retiro Park [the lush

> central park of Madrid], is occupied by forty students, men and women .... Ortega comes into the class with a leather folder in his hand. He takes a small book out of it: it is one of the dialogues of Plato, the "Theaetetus"; before beginning to read it, he explains to the students, as a brief introduction, what his course in philosophy is going to be like.... <u>The master's words, clear, precise, elegant, produce a strange emotion</u>. The students try to take notes in their notebooks; but soon they listen with absorption, their pens hovering over the paper, to the marvel of that philosophical exposition clothed in such richness of images and metaphors. It seems that we are witnessing, not the teaching of a magisterial class, but *the progress of a dramatic theory whose protagonist is the philospher's very life*.[15]

The "Jericho" method is why the reader of Ortega needs to be patient and follow the threads of his thought. The docile, the teachable reader will be rewarded as is also true in the reading of many other authors. The reader who already has an agenda will, of course, refuse to follow the process in good faith and dismiss it as nonsense. All master teachers deserve students who are in good faith. Now, we are ready, in good faith, to expectantly enter the pages of Ortega's lectures entitled *What is Philosophy?*, first given in 1929. That good faith will be rewarded because Ortega the master teacher, unlike many other academic writers, both preached and practiced the rubric that "[i]n philosophy, <u>clarity is courtesy</u>."[16]

Now, like those pleasantly surprised students back on an early Madrid morning in the early twentieth century, we are privileged in the early twenty-first century to glimpse some of that philosophical genius as contained in Ortega's lectures entitled *What is Philosophy?*

CHAPTER 2   SURPASSING MODERN PHILOSOPHY

In our ordinary speech, we tend to think of "modern" as what is contemporary. But, when we survey the history of philosophy, we give a very different historical meaning to the term "modern philosophy." Modern philosophy in the context of Ortega's lectures is that philosophical worldview introduced by René Descartes in the 17th century and which culminates with the full-fledged philosophy of Idealism of Immanuel Kant in the 18th century. The philosophy of Idealism is what Ortega is initiated into and absorbs in his studies in Germany, what he then wrestles with from the inside, and what he ultimately surpasses. Ortega viewed this surpassing of Idealism as his personal mission and destiny, the mission that put him at the "height of the times." All of these terms--"mission," "destiny," and, as we have already seen, "height of the times"--are carefully chosen terms whose sense will be shown to be essential to Ortega's own philosophical system.

But, what is so important about modern philosophy or Idealism? Can wrestling with this philosophical current really be worth all of the trouble? Doesn't it all seem so very academic and hence very unimportant for our lives? Ortega was never one to waste his efforts on the trivial. We need to see why surpassing the Idealism in which he immersed himself while in Germany was the life mission of a very passionate intellectual who did not believe in pouring his life into trifles or mere academic erudition.

Ortega describes what Idealism signifies for the heroic philosophic quest to attempt to describe the universe that he defines as "all that there is" ("*todo lo que hay*")[17]:

> Since Descartes, in effect, philosophy, in taking its first step, takes a direction opposite to our mental habits, walks in the opposite direction from the natural flow of life and distances itself with uniformly accelerated movement, to the point that in Leibniz, in Kant, in Fichte, or in Hegel, philosophy becomes the philosophy of the world seen in reverse, a magnificent, anti-natural doctrine that cannot be understood without previous initiation, a doctrine for the initiated, a secret wisdom, an esoteric knowledge. Thought has swallowed the world: things have become mere ideas.[18]

This situation is intolerable to the passionate philosopher for whom philosophy is a vital yet sportive[19] necessity, a necessity rooted in human flourishing. Such a philosopher cannot be satisfied with the esoteric knowledge of Idealism, which must first be absorbed and digested, as Ortega did in his studies, and then surpassed by a new generation.

In truly coming to grips with Idealism, we first see its historical value, its contribution to the history of philosophy:

> The superiority of Idealism derives from its having discovered something whose mode of being is radically different from that of all other things. . . . [Thinking and reflection] consist fundamentally in being-for-itself, in becoming aware of itself.[20]

This innovation and discovery of Idealism is in contrast to the ancient world view[21] in which things ("*cosas*") remained exterior to the self:

Ancient man .... lives on the basis of things and only the cosmos of bodies exists for him. ... Greek ideas are molded by a reality composed of exterior and corporeal things.[22]

It is surprising to us that, for the Greeks, this corporal or physical nature of reality even included the soul itself as a material object.[23] Thus, Ortega notes that "[t]he Greek has not discovered the soul as a result of the intimate examination of himself, but rather finds the soul external to himself as a quasi-corporal entity."[24]

In contrast to this ancient world view, Idealism does not "begin from the reality of the exterior world: all bodies, as many as surround us, including our own body, are suspect in their pretense of existing in themselves, independently of our thinking them."[25] Idealism has discovered that the thinking self is the only thing immune to doubt. Hence, all other things become anchored in the thoughts of the self. Reality derives from the ideas of a thinking self. The magnificent discovery of subjectivity by Idealism results in a system which takes this discovery to its apparently logical but erroneous conclusion.[26]

In his *History of Philosophy*, Julián Marías, whose approach to the history of philosophy was inspired by Ortega, describes the Idealism that began with Descartes in the following way.[27] The description is worth quoting at length because of its clarity (of which Descartes himself would approve!) and because getting a firm grasp on Idealism is a prerequisite to understanding the philosophical quest of Ortega:

The thesis of idealism is in direct opposition to metaphysical realism. As represented in ancient Greece and the Middle Ages, realism is the belief that the things [in Spanish, *cosas*] have a being of their own, that the ego exists merely as one thing among others, and that true reality consists of the things, *res*. To be means *to be* (or exist) *separately, to have a being independent of me.* Idealism, on the contrary, is the belief that the ego has no sure knowledge of anything other than itself (the *cogito*); that I know the things only while I am seeing them, touching them, thinking of them, desiring them, and so forth. (The word *cogitatio* does not mean only *thought*; it also includes all mental processes.) In other words, I know the things only while I have dealings with them and witness them. I do not and cannot know what the things are like when they are apart from me—not even if they exist in me, since I know nothing of them without being present. That is, the things appear as existing or being *for me*; thus, they are provisionally *ideas* of mine and the reality that corresponds to them is an ideal reality. The being of things is based on the ego, and resembles ideas on the part of the ego: this is idealism.[28]

In the ancient world view, man naturally encounters external things or bodies. In his excellent introductory book on Ortega, British scholar Andrew Dobson uses the term "realism" to refer to the ancient world view, as does Ortega himself and also Marías in the above quoted excerpt.[29] In contrast, in the "modern" world view of Idealism, external things become man's ideas—the things around him now exist as thoughts in his mind. **This unnatural turn to an extreme subjectivity is what Ortega seeks to surpass.**

But why is this philosophical turn to subjectivity so problematic to Ortega? What problems does this unnatural turn to all-encompassing subjectivity create for him and for us? Is this just an arcane problem for those whose leisurely hobby is the history of philosophy? Or is it a real, live practical problem for us? A recent book by *New York Times* columnist David Brooks gives us a very current view of the problem.[30] Brooks recounts how rationalism as a problematic child of modern or Idealist philosophy still distorts our view of ourselves and of the world. It is noteworthy, if not somewhat surprising, that the problems arising from Idealism, the problems with which Ortega first wrestled in the early 20th century, are still seen as problematic today at the beginning of the 21st century:

> [D]uring the seventeenth century, scientists and technologists created new forms of machinery and new ways to think about society. Great investigators began to dissect and understand their world. The metaphor, "the world is a machine," began to replace the [ancient, classical] metaphor, "the world is a living organism.". . . . This rationalist mode of thought is omnipresent and seems natural and inevitable. The rationalist tradition proved seductive. . . . But it does contain certain limitations and biases. This mode of thought is reductionist .... It is purposeful rather than playful. It values the sort of knowledge that can be put into words and numbers over the sort of knowledge that cannot . . . . and undervalues the importance of specific contexts.[31]

Brooks as a social commentator is pointing out the problem with the rationalism of Descartes,[32] a rationalism that changed the qualitatively rich world of the ancient Greek into the quantitatively defined world of Newton. Ortega's task of surpassing Idealism is still very much relevant today because the inadequate and misleading assumptions of Idealism still influence our ways of thinking about human life and society, as Brooks documents in his book. And, if Ortega's task is still relevant, then certainly the philosophical response of Ortega in taking up this task is still relevant, although Brooks does not refer to Ortega in this particular book.

    For Ortega, the modern philosophy of Idealism with its rationalism, however much he may wish to surpass it, is still very much in keeping with the philosophical passion for truth and clarity, for getting to the bottom of things. As Ortega notes,

"Philosophy is an enormous appetite for transparency and a resolute will for the clarity of midday."[33]

That passion for clarity and transparency is an essential part of Ortega's definition of philosophy. This philosophical passion is what makes philosophy a form of "intellectual heroism" with a "frenetic" character.[34] The intellectual heroism of Idealism boldly went so far as to give us the counterintuitive view that the reality of objects consists of the thoughts in our minds. The task of our time, according to Ortega and to others, is to take the historic and essential discovery of subjectivity by the Idealists and move beyond its limits in order to advance philosophy's grasp of reality. That advance will have very practical social effects as noted in David Brooks' book.

What is at stake is that Idealism, if left unsurpassed, leaves us with an inaccurate depiction of reality and of our lives. For philosophy, that predicament of inaccuracy is unacceptable. As the famous historian of philosophy, the late Frederick Copleston wrote, for Ortega, philosophy "is therefore, not a body of propositions which can be handed on, but a personal activity, the activity of striving after clarity about the human situation. And, as a personal activity, it is, and must be, constantly renewed. Each genuine philosopher must do the work again, so to speak."[35] Ortega, after having immersed himself in Idealism, saw the urgency of doing the work again.

CHAPTER 3 CHRISTIANITY AND THE DISCOVERY OF SUBJECTIVITY

Before moving on to see Ortega's own distinctive philosophical response to Idealism, it is quite interesting to consider Ortega's comments on the role of Christian thought in the discovery of subjectivity, comments with a special emphasis on the contribution of Augustine of Hippo. Since Ortega himself devotes several pages to this Christian "excursus," we would do well not to ignore it, especially since the issue is so significant for the history of Western philosophy. Remember that what we are about in this book is illustrating how Ortega struggles with and seeks to advance the history of Western philosophy.

The Orteguian excursus on Christianity and the philosophical discovery of subjectivity is found in Chapter ("Lección") 8 of *What is Philosophy? (¿Qué es filosofía?* or *QEF*); the page references that follow are to *QEF*. I will translate and comment as I go forward. First, Ortega discusses Christianity as one of two sources for the discovery of subjectivity:

> The discovery of subjectivity has two deep historical roots: one negative and one positive. The negative root is skepticism; the positive root is Christianity. Neither one alone would have been able to produce such a result (pp. 144-45; English trans. at 170).

But, according to Ortega, ancient Greek skepticism alone was not enough to ensure the discovery of our human subjectivity. For that discovery, a new notion of the divine was necessary—the divine as transcendent, not as dwelling in the things of nature (p.

147; English trans. at 173). In order to encounter this transcendent God, the Christian must nullify nature and enter into himself:

> In order to be with God one must begin by virtually voiding all that is cosmic and earthly, to treat it as non-existent given that, in effect, compared to God, it is nothing. And this is how, in order for the soul to approach God, in its urgent approach to the divine, in order to save itself, the soul will accomplish the same thing as the skeptic does with his methodical doubt. . . . God and, before Him, the solitary soul. . . . It is not an accident that St. Augustine is the first thinker, who was able to glimpse the fact of consciousness and of being as intimacy, and it is also not an accident that he was the first one to discover that what cannot be doubted is our doubt. It is remarkable that the founder of the Christian ideology and the founder of modern philosophy completely coincide in their first step (p. 148; English trans. at 173-74).

In this way, Ortega points to Augustine as a precursor of Descartes, who himself was, from outward indications at least, quite Catholic.[36] Yet, Ortega also emphasizes that it is "false to affirm that Descartes was already in St. Augustine."[37] Ortega distinguishes between Augustine the great religious thinker and Descartes the great philosopher: "St. Augustine was a genius of religious sensibility; through his religious intuition St. Augustine comes to discover the reflective self . . . but he lacked the stroke of felicitous, visionary insight that led [Descartes] to turn the entire ancient worldview upside down and to lay the foundation for idealism."[38]

Nevertheless, as Ortega's disciple, Julián Marías wrote, the role of Augustine is still significant:

St. Augustine's [354-430 A.D.] thought contains something characteristic not only of Christianity but also of the modern epoch: **intimacy**. We have seen how he bases his philosophy on the inner man. He asks man to enter the interior of his own soul in order to find himself, and with himself, God. This is the great lesson which St. Anselm [1033-1109 A.D.] will learn first, and through him all Western mysticism. . . . The *Confessions* represents man's first attempt to approach himself. Until the advent of idealism--that is, until the seventeenth century--no one will achieve anything comparable. And when modern man, guided by Descartes, returns to himself and remains alone with his ego, St. Augustine will again acquire profound influence.[39]

In addition, it is very interesting to note how Ortega takes pleasure in pointing out the common ground concerning individual subjectivity that is found in both Christianity and modern philosophy, to the consternation of some ideologues both in the Christian camp and in the camp of modern philosophy. We see in this case how Ortega, although from all indications not a practicing Catholic as an adult, retained an even-handed appreciation for the great contributions of Christianity to Western thought and did not exhibit the extreme anti-clerical mentality of some secular thinkers: "This possibility [of the influence of the transcendence of the Christian God on the rise of modern philosophy] unsettles the Christians and irritates the anti-Christians, the 'moderns.' "[40]

Of course, not all Christians then and now find this historical conjunction of Christianity and modern philosophy unsettling; and not all modern philosophers were or are irritated by the historical confluence of Christian ideas and modern philosophy. Ortega seems to be aiming his critique at the ideological extremists in both camps who find any mutual influence between the camps quite alarming. Yet, as we have seen, Descartes himself found no problem in reconciling Catholicism and his new philosophic method. It is also noteworthy that Ortega himself insists that it is the distinctive Christian conception of the transcendent God that made modern philosophy possible when he says that "only the Christian" God made the leap to subjectivity possible.[41]

Any attempt to advance the course of Western philosophy requires, according to Ortega, wrestling with and truly understanding the preceding philosophical tradition and its influences. It is thus quite appropriate for Ortega to address and describe the role of Christianity in the rise of modern philosophy and to fairly give credit where credit is due to the formative influence of Christian ideas.[42]

CHAPTER 4   STARTING AGAIN

Earlier in this book, I noted Ortega's determination to surpass Idealism. It is worth taking time to read Ortega's own articulation of why this task is necessary:

> Idealism has gotten to the point of blocking up the sources of our vital energies, of totally weakening the very springs and means of living. Because it [Idealism] has almost convinced man in all seriousness, that is to say, vitally, that everything that surrounds him consists of himself and what he thinks.[43]

What Ortega describes above is an excessively abstract intellectualism that is not true to life as lived. Because of this preoccupation to be true to life as lived, it is no accident that Ortega's philosophy is often seen as a form of "vitalism." Yet, Julián Marías rightly insists that lumping Ortega with earlier "philosophies of life" and forms of philosophical vitalism, such as that of Bergson, is simply missing the boat. **What Ortega will contribute that is new and daring is to address life as a radical reality and not to impose preconceived narrow ideas on the radical reality of life, ideas such as biological life (Bergson) or vitality (Nietzsche).**[44] Thus, to label and pigeonhole Ortega as just one more "vitalist" derails us from the quest of understanding his thought and trivializes his achievements.

Ortega formulates the challenge and the problem in terms of the ego (in Spanish, "*el yo*"). On the one hand, to advance philosophically, it makes no sense to return to the naiveté of the ancient world view which ignored the ego as intimacy and viewed the ego as one more thing among many other things in the world. On the other hand, it is intolerable, as we have seen, to remain stuck with the ego of Idealism which is, in a sense, stuck with itself and within itself—a state designated by the densely packed Spanish term *"ensimismamiento"* which can be literally translated as the state of "being-within-oneself." Thus, neither the ancient world view of naïve realism nor the modern world view of Idealism is any longer acceptable.[45]

With Ortega, and many of his contemporaries in philosophy, we turn to the contemporary world view. Ortega offers a distinctive philosophical expression of the contemporary world view also seen in the work of Husserl, Heidegger, and others. What we are about in this book is appreciating the distinctive contribution of Ortega to the contemporary world view, a contribution that is in many ways superior in its clarity, vigor, and comprehensiveness to the other contemporary alternatives. In addition, Ortega offers a system of thought not associated with embarrassing political associations and pronouncements, such as those of Heidegger during the Hitler era, associations which cannot be completely discounted in evaluating a philosopher's thought.

In Lesson (Chapter) IX of *¿Qué es filosofía?* (*What is Philosophy?*), Ortega indeed tells us what is involved in the task of philosophizing in general—which is, after all, the theme of the book—in the course of his discussing in these pages the specific context of surpassing Idealism. Ortega will show us what, in general, philosophy is by philosophizing in very concrete and specific terms in the course of this book. He explains philosophizing by actually philosophizing before our eyes.

First of all, philosophy as the quest for truth is preceded by the human desire for a new and better truth:

Truth descends only on the one who seeks it, who longs for it and already carries in himself the pre-existing intellectual space in which the truth can lodge. . . . With a skeptical sense and in order to stigmatize truth, it is said that desire is the father of truth. This [view] is, as all skepticism is, a perfect absurdity or nonsense. If a particular truth is desired, it is desired if it is, in effect, truth. The desire for truth transcends oneself, leaves oneself behind, and goes out to find the truth. Man is very much aware of when he desires a truth and when he desires only to deceive himself, that is, when he desires what is false.[46]

As a result, philosophy is a mission; and, for Ortega, the mission of his time—"the theme of our time"—is the surpassing of Idealism.[47] This view of philosophy is an expression of Ortega's view of time not as "what clocks measure" but rather time as "task, mission, innovation."[48] So, at this point, we can affirm, thus far, that, for Ortega, *philosophy is the passionate search for the truth about all that there is, a search so passionate that it is in the nature of a mission intent on surpassing what is incomplete or erroneous by pursuing the innovation that leads us closer to what is true. Notice that this surpassing of what is incomplete requires genuine appreciation of what is true in prior thought.*

How is this mission to be accomplished in Ortega's time? How is Idealism to be surpassed? To those readers already familiar with Heidegger's classic *Sein und Zeit* (*Being and Time*), the way forward from Idealism will seem familiar, although all indications are that Ortega named this route independently of Heidegger:

You are invited to abandon obeisance to the most venerable, persistent, and firm concept in the tradition of our thinking: the concept of being ["*ser*"]. I declare "checkmate" to the being of Plato, of Aristotle, of Leibniz, of Kant, and, it is clear, also to that of Descartes.[49]

As to the issue of who was first in articulating the need to revise the traditional concept of being in a revolutionary, existentialist manner, Ortega himself claimed that his analysis originated independently of Heidegger.[50] Regardless of who published or thought what first, the reality is that these two contemporaries raised very similar issues at about the same time. What is key here is that both Heidegger and Ortega very explicitly and self-consciously wrestled with the great Western philosophical tradition in order to explore further and revise further the traditional concept of Being. The lesson here for us is to enter that great philosophical tradition and to take it seriously and to surpass it. That lesson of surpassing the history of philosophy is an integral part of what philosophy is. There can be no philosophizing without an explicit or implicit history of philosophy; and, of course, the more explicit the likelier it is that the end result will be a true advance from the past.

As a genuine philosopher, Ortega starts his analysis from the achievement of Descartes. Ortega submits, to use his own image, the insight of Descartes to philosophical surgery.[51] Ortega focuses with laser-like intensity on the famous Cartesian phrase: "*Cogito ergo, sum*" ("I think, therefore I am"/ "*Je pense, donc je suis*"). Ortega lavishly celebrates the great insight of Descartes: the discovery of thought, *cogitatio* (in Spanish, *pensamiento*) as indicating my existence:

> My thought is what is *for* me thought: I am, and I exist to the extent and so much as and only because I think that I am and as I think that I am. This is the innovation that Idealism sought to bring to the world and is the true spiritualism; the rest is nothing but magic.[52]

The next crucial point is that, after Descartes comes to this marvelous insight linking thought (or better and dynamically stated, the activity of thinking) and the ego, Descartes falters and surrenders to the ancient Greek world view: namely, viewing the being of the ego as a static thing, although thought or thinking is not a static thing but rather is "an active appearing to oneself and giving of being to oneself":[53]

> [For Descartes] the ego is not thought, but a thing ["*cosa*" in Spanish] about which thought is an attribute, a manifestation, a phenomenon. We have fallen again into the static being of Greek ontology. In the very same sentence, in the very same act by which Descartes discovers a new world for us, he hides away and voids this new world. He has the intuition, the vision of being-for-itself, but conceives this being-for-itself as a being of [static] substance in the Greek mode.[54]

Of course, we can certainly forgive the undoubted genius of Descartes for this clinging to the ancient world view. Our own humility tells us that we too will cling, often without realizing it, to modes of thought that our best insights are telling us to abandon. To philosophize is a gradual process because we humans are creatures of habit. We have for so long supported ourselves on various unstated and unconscious assumptions that we will always find ourselves needing to uncover and revise those assumptions one by one (*paulatim*, to use an apt Latin word).

    With Ortega, we are now going to amiably escape the old Greek world view as the Greeks "will stop being our pedagogues, will start to be our friends. We are going to converse with them; we are going to contradict them in what is most essential."[55]

    Idealism then takes this ego as thing and substances and faces the dilemma of exterior reality: is that exterior reality outside the ego-as-substance or inside the ego-as-substance? Idealism answers that question by saying that reality is nothing more than the "contents of consciousness."[56] Ortega boldly puts his finger on the error of Idealism which assumed simplistically that there were only two choices: reality inside the mind or reality outside the mind. He ascribes this error to failing to remain scrupulously true to the meaning of the process of representation. Representation of anything always involves the one representing and what is represented. The two aspects cannot be blithely merged by an equivocal, non-specific use of the term "representation" that ignores these two aspects of the one representing and what is represented.[57]

What then, at the end of the day, is the error of Idealism? Its error lies in trying to make substances or things ("*cosas*") out of the representing ego and the represented exterior reality so that exterior reality simply becomes the contents of my own consciousness. If we drop the ancient prejudice in favor of imposing the categories of things and substances on lived experience, we come closer to the truth: the ego and exterior reality exist in mutual interdependence. They are not two separate substances which require us to have either the ego swallow up exterior reality or to have exterior reality exist beyond our consciousness.

The solution lies in allowing the ego and objects to exist inseparably, in immediate relationship, even if we distinguish between the two dimensions of our existence.[58] The ego and the world exist "in active correlation" and in "intimacy."[59] We can see here the force of Ortega's most famous philosophical dictum: "I am I and my circumstance."[60] This dictum signifies that the radical reality "is not my existence . . . but rather my **coexistence** with the world."[61]

What does this theoretical insight mean for my life? I have to go to the eloquence of the original:

> The truth is that I exist with this world of mine and in my world—and I consist in occupying myself with this world of mine, in seeing it, in imagining it, in thinking it, in loving it, in hating it, in being sad or joyful in it and because of it, in moving myself in it, in transforming it and suffering in it. Nothing of this would be possible for me if the world did not coexist with me, before me, around me, pressing me, manifesting itself, inspiring me, upsetting me.[62]

This reality of coexistence is nothing more than "my life":

> not my ego alone, not my hermetically sealed consciousness, these things are already interpretations, the idealist interpretation. What is given is "my life," and my life is above all a finding myself in the world; and not in a vague manner but rather in this particular world, . . . in this instant, doing what I am doing in it, in this theatrical piece of my world, [in which] I am philosophizing [referring to the literal theater, the hall, in which Ortega is lecturing in 1929].[63]

In conclusion, Ortega announces that to philosophize is to meditate about and to define "that primary reality that we call 'our life.' "[64] As Ortega notes, this definition of philosophy abandons the old abstractions and opens for us a new horizon that urgently touches what is most personal and intimate for each of us.

The classic and most famous expression by Ortega of this primary reality, the philosophical dictum just noted above, is found in fuller form in his very first published book *Meditations on Quixote* (1914), as follows:

> I am I and my circumstance, and, if I do not save it, I do not save myself. *Benefac loco illi quo natus es* ["Do good to that place where you have been born"], we read in the Bible.

And in the Platonic School this is given as the project of all culture: "save the appearances," the phenomena. That is to say, search for the meaning of what surrounds us. . . . There is nothing on the globe through which there does not pass some divine nerve: the difficulty lies in getting to it, and in our allowing it to penetrate us. . . . Nothing impedes heroism--which is the activity of the spirit--as much as to consider it limited to certain specific spheres of life. It is certain that there exists everywhere—underground—the possibility of heroism and that every man, if he strikes with vigor the earth on which he walks, should expect a fountain to erupt. For Moses the Hero, every rock is a spring.[65]

In this 1914 description, Ortega captures the vital significance of his philosophizing: we come to a heightened understanding and awareness of the drama and heroism of our own individual lives. Thus, in seeking to define philosophy, we must add another component to our definition: philosophy, at its best, serves as a guide to a greater, practical appreciation of the often hidden potentialities of our lives.

CHAPTER 5   WHAT IS LIVING?

Having established "life" as the new focus of philosophical analysis, Ortega proceeds to describe this radical reality. In place of "being" defined as a self-subsistent, independent thing ("*cosa*") as prior philosophy did, now "being" has the character of "interdependence of the ego and the things" around me so that "to be is to need, one from another."[66] Thus, "what is primary in the universe is 'my living' and all else exists or does not exist in my life, within it."[67]

The task now is, as Ortega says, "to break in new concepts."[68] First, life is immediate and personal—"it is what is immediate to each one."[69] The life of the sane person is the life about which one is conscious in contrast to the existence of a rock which lacks self-consciousness, or to the life of the madman whose life no longer belongs to himself because he has lost awareness of it.[70]

Second, life involves being occupied with and concerned with the other: "all living is to coexist with a circumstance."[71] At this point, Ortega, the master of metaphor, gives us a classical allusion: our relation to the world around us is not optional, is not subsequent to our living, rather the ego and the circumstance are like the Greco-Roman *dioscuri*, the pagan divinities who always acted together, the "*dii consentes*, the unanimous gods," who were inseparable.[72]

Third, life happens *in medias res* ("in the midst of things," as the epic poets would say)—we enter the stage of life in the middle of the play, a play which we do not choose or design to suit our tastes and preferences. As Ortega puts it, with another metaphor: "Our life begins by being the perpetual surprise of existing, without our prior consent, as shipwrecked people, on an unforeseen globe."[73] Thus, it is foolish to waste time complaining that things are not as we would have wished. Ortega also compares life to a person being pushed on stage without any prior preparation so that life is improvisation.[74]

Fourth, this life given to us is inherently problematic. Our task is to improvise a solution: "what is given to us, life, is a problem that we ourselves need to resolve."[75] Thus, life is responsibility. The moral character of that life is the next step to consider; but both the good and the bad must, of necessity, face the challenges with comparatively better or worse solutions.

Fifth, within the constraints of the stage of our circumstances, we do possess freedom, a freedom which operates within the "fate" of our circumstances so that life has "a certain margin" and comes "with a vital horizon of possibilities" which gives us freedom.[76] Ortega compares the reality of our freedom within constraints to the freedom and creativity of the poet who creates precisely within and through the strict requirements of poetic rhyme and meter.[77]

Sixth, life is then, in sum, "constantly deciding what we are going to be."[78] As a result, our life is intrinsically a collision with the future. Thus, "life is futurity, it is what it is not yet."[79]

How then do these traits affect us who are living now? Philosophy first emerges most dramatically with Socrates seeking to find the good life. The question of the good life is inherent in seeking to make sense of our existence. Ortega himself viewed as most desirable the writing of the memoirs of a thoughtful human being, who could then share the wisdom and insights for living that governed his daily life: "We want, in gratitude, to return to life what life has given us, or what we have wrenched out of life; to return it after having meditated about it and distilled it."[80] There is wisdom for living found in the Orteguian analysis of life. I suggest that a person who takes the Orteguian analysis of living seriously will adopt an outlook that assesses one's own life, not by engaging in comparisons with others, but primarily by searching for one's unique contribution to the world. Conformity is not the route to take since each one's life is personal and intimate and belongs to each one, not to others.

In addition, we have to take our circumstances seriously. We must recognize that the where and when of our lives are an inseparable part of who we are. Of course, this circumstantiality does not mean that we are at the mercy of where we were born or where we happen to live now. Travel and immigration, whether temporary or permanent, may be necessary to extract our true life project. Although Ortega embraced Spain as his life project, he spent years in study in Germany and later in exile in order to carry that project forward. Others may be called to leave their birthplace altogether. Again, circumstances are crucial to our self-identity. We need to choose them wisely, including the individuals with whom we associate, who are a crucial part of our circumstance. When the circumstances in which we find ourselves are bad, then we have to change them right there where we are or seek another set of circumstances altogether.

We also cannot spend time bemoaning our handicaps, limits, and bad inheritance, whether physical, intellectual, social, or emotional. Everyone comes onto the stage limited and constrained. The urgency is to start addressing the problems which make up life. The goal is not a life without problems, something which would not be recognizable as life at all, but rather to face problems with a life project. We have the freedom to fashion a small diamond out of the coal given to us. Ortega compared this freedom to the metaphor Nietzsche used to describe the artist as "the man who dances in chains."[81] Even in prison itself, people can flourish and make their mark, as people from Boethius to the Vietnamese cardinal who spent years in a Communist prison have shown.[82]

Another trait of the person who lives the life described by Ortega is a focus on the future. We have to decide what we are going to do, rather than waste time on seeking vengeance or on brooding. The best response to past disappointments and tragedies is to decide differently in the future.

CONCLUSION: WHAT THEN IS PHILOSOPHY?

That is the question with which we began; that is the very title of Ortega's book which we have been exploring. First, we begin with the radical reality that all things are found within my life and that all things have a use or serviceability for my life.[83] In philosophy, we choose to take certain things in our life and set them apart for the sake of contemplation; we strip them of serviceability for my life and wish to look at them apart from the demands of my living.

Ortega goes on: "But this—finding in something what it itself has absolutely, and to cut off all other partial interest of mine toward it, to cease using it, to not wish it to serve me, but rather that I serve it as an impartial pupil [or eye] so that it can see itself, find itself, and be itself and for itself—this, this . . . is this not love?"[84]

Thus, we are back to the old Platonic conception of philosophy as the erotic love of wisdom, but now the objects of contemplation are first taken out of my life and are not things that exist apart from my life. The old concept of being as a thing thus reemerges, but now as an abstraction from my life, from the interdependence of the ego and the world. In this way, the definition of philosophy still includes the traditional experience of a loving contemplation.

Moreover, we see that philosophy is what the philosopher does, precisely by so taking an object and intentionally setting it apart for contemplation. "The being of philosophy is what the philosopher does, to philosophize is a way of living . . . . It is an 'unliving' ["desvivir"]—an 'unliving' for the sake of all that there is, for the Universe—a making in oneself a place and a space where the Universe can be known and known again."[85] Thus, philosophy is a way of living; and so it was also for the ancient Greeks for whom the first philosophy books were the biographies of the first Seven Sages.[86]

What has this philosophizing done for us in these pages written by Ortega over 80 years ago? It has uncovered for us the truth of our living *now* (remember the Greek term for truth, *aletheia*,[87] "revealing" or "uncovering"):

> [H]uman life is constant anticipation and pre-formation of the future . . . . [but] that future is not just any future, but the possible "now," and that past is the past until *now*, not the past of someone who lived one hundred years ago. Do you see? "Now" is our time, our world, our life.[88]

What then are we to do with this "now" that is always before us as long as we are living? "[T]he role of fate [or of what is determined] that intervenes in our life . . . is like [our] falling into a trap. Yet this trap does not kill us, it grants to [our] life a margin of decision-making and always allows us, from the imposed situation, from destiny, to give an elegant solution and to forge a beautiful life."[89]

So, then, let us live in the full Orteguian sense of the term and not drift; for as the Finnish proverb warns us, "Only dead fish follow the stream."

Author Oswald Sobrino

holds an M.A. in Theology, an M.A. in Economics, and a J.D. He is fluent in Spanish, and teaches both biblical studies and Latin. In the past, he has also taught economics. Madrid, Spain, the home of Ortega y Gasset, is one of his favorite cities. His website *Logos* is located at www.catholicanalysis.blogspot.com. This book will hopefully be the first in a series of short books on Ortega's writings. You can contact him at sobrino95@gmail.com.

Other recent books by the same author:

5 Lessons from Augustine (also available online; a brief book on the *Confessions* of St. Augustine of Hippo)

Suggested Reading and Bibliography

Artis, Aderemi. "Descartes, Luther, and the Fifth Lateran Council." *An Anthology of Philosophical Studies*. Edited by Patricia Hanna et al. Vol. 5. ATINER, 2011. Available at http://www.umflint.edu/philosophy/faculty_research.htm#artis_journals .

Brooks, David. *The Social Animal: The Hidden Sources of Love, Character, and Achievement*. New York: Random House, 2011. Brooks is a *New York Times* columnist.

Copleston, S.J., Frederick. *A History of Philosophy, Volume IV: From Descartes to Leibniz*. New York: Image Books, 1994. This series is, in my view, the standard history of philosophy in English.

Copleston, S.J., Frederick. *Philosophers and Philosophies*. New York: Barnes & Noble Books, 1976. Contains an interesting article on Ortega.

Crow, John A. *Spain: The Root and the Flower, An Interpretation of Spain and the Spanish People*, 3rd ed. Berkeley: University of California Press, 1985. As noted in the text, this author makes a massive misjudgment concerning Ortega.

Dobson, Andrew. *An Introduction to the Politics and Philosophy of José Ortega y Gasset*. Cambridge Iberian and Latin American Studies. Cambridge Univ. Press, 1989. Dobson is a careful, conscientious scholar.

Holmes, Oliver. "José Ortega y Gasset." *Stanford Encyclopedia of Philosophy* § 1.6: Summer 2011 Edition. Edited by Edward N. Zalta. Available at http://plato.stanford.edu/archives/sum2011/entries/gasset/ . This article is extensive, excellent, and recent.

Marías, Julián. *History of Philosophy*. Translated by Stanley Applebaum and Clarence C. Strowbridge. New York: Dover Publications, 1967. This book is a welcome addition to the library of anyone interested in philosophy.

Marías, Julián. *José Ortega y Gasset: Circumstance and Vocation*. Translated by Frances M. López-Morillas. Norman: Univ. of Oklahoma Press, 1970. This work provides excellent scholarly background to Ortega's circumstances.

Ortega y Gasset, José. *Meditaciones del Quijote*. Madrid: Revista de Occidente, 1957; originally published 1914. English translation: *Meditations on Quixote*. Translated by Evelyn Rugg and Diego Marín. New York: W.W. Norton, 1961.

Ortega y Gasset, José. *¿Qué es filosofía?* Edited by Paulino Garagorri. Madrid: Revista de Occidente en Alianza Editorial, 1989. This text is the original Spanish, with some additional relevant material. Primary source for my book.

Ortega y Gasset, José. *Sobre la razón histórica*. Edited by Paulino Garagorri. Madrid: Revista de Occidente en Alianza Editorial, 1979. An English translation is available online: *Historical Reason*. Translated by Philip W. Silver. New York: W.W. Norton, 1984. Available at http://www.questia.com/PM.qst?a=o&d=105087575#.

Ortega y Gasset, José. *What is Philosophy?* Translated by Mildred Adams. New York: W.W. Norton, 1964. This reference is to the Norton Library edition. I highly recommend reading this book to understand my own book and, more importantly, to fully appreciate Ortega.

Rodríguez Huéscar, Antonio. *Semblanza de Ortega* ("Biographical Sketch of Ortega"). Edited by José Lasaga. Barcelona: Editorial Anthropos, 1994. Excellent portrayal of Ortega, but in Spanish.

NOTES

[1] Yet, even the well-known Hispanist John Crow, who taught in the United States, made the tragic and frankly surprising intellectual error of refusing to see Ortega as a philosopher and instead patronizingly labelled him as a mere "sensationalist journalist." John A. Crow, *Spain: The Root and the Flower, An Interpretation of Spain and the Spanish People* 3rd ed. (Berkeley: University of California Press, 1985), p. 274. So sympathy for Hispanic culture alone—a sympathy amply displayed by Prof. Crow—is not enough to lead to an appreciation of Ortega's true significance as a philosopher. What is also needed is an appreciation of the history of philosophy itself combined with a serious and open-minded reading of Ortega's philosophical writings. This book, like others, seeks to be the catalyst for such a serious reading of Ortega the philosopher. Such a reading is not primarily a foray into Hispanic culture, but is rather a foray into serious philosophy that is urgently relevant for all cultures and for all human beings of whatever ethnic background.

[2] Julián Marías, *History of Philosophy*, trans. Stanley Applebaum and Clarence C. Strowbridge (New York: Dover Publications, 1967), p. 468. Hereafter cited as "Marías, *History*" or simply as "*History*."

[3] Ortega y Gasset, José. Trans. Mildred Adams. *What Is Philosophy?* New York: W.W. Norton, 1964. **For the understandable convenience of those who do not read Spanish or possess the Spanish original of this work, I will add, in my footnotes and sometimes in the main text, cross-references to the above English translation to accompany my own translations, so that readers will be able to go to the full English translation to verify and grasp the context of a passage quoted by me.** I strongly recommend that English-only readers make use of the Mildred Adams translation, mentioned above. Note that the Latin abbreviation "Id." in the following footnotes means that the reference is to the same source given in the preceding footnote. (Some of you may be more familiar with the longer abbreviation "Ibid." which performs the same function.)

[4] Ortega y Gasset, *¿Qué es filosofía?* (Madrid: Revista de Occidente en Alianza Editorial, 1989), in the *Works of José Ortega y Gasset*, edited by Paulino Garagorri. **Hereafter cited as "Ortega, *QEF*, ed. Garagorri" or, most often, as simply "*QEF*."**

[5] Julián Marías, *José Ortega y Gasset: Circumstance and Vocation*, trans. Frances M. López-Morillas (Norman: Univ. of Oklahoma Press, 1970), p. 213. Henceforth cited as "Marías, *Circumstance*" or simply as "*Circumstance*." This work is especially valuable in tracing the beginnings of Ortega's thought in his early writings, especially the seminal *Meditations on Quixote* (1914). Ever the thorough scholar, Marías devotes the first two chapters of *Circumstance* to separate, detailed treatments of the Spanish and wider European historical and cultural ambience that influenced Ortega. Clearly, my short book cannot even begin to duplicate that level of historical detail and erudition. It is also of interest that Julián Marías was a practicing Catholic enthusiastic about Ortega, although Ortega no longer practiced the Catholic faith of his youthful education at the hands of the Jesuits. There may be a lesson there for those who like to put barriers between thinkers.

[6] Marías, *Circumstance*, pp. 189-93.

[7] Marías, *History of Philosophy*, pp. 442-43; Holmes, Oliver, "José Ortega y Gasset", *The Stanford Encyclopedia of Philosophy*, § 1.6 (Summer 2011 Edition), Edward N. Zalta (ed.), URL = http://plato.stanford.edu/archives/sum2011/entries/gasset/ [hereafter cited as Holmes, *SEP*].

[8] Holmes, *SEP*, § 1.6.

[9] It should be noted that Heidegger today has a mixed reputation because of his support of Hitler during the Nazi era in Germany. To his credit, Ortega never allied himself with nor, to my knowledge, ever endorsed any form of totalitarianism, whether of the left or of the right. In that sense, Ortega's achievements remain untainted when compared to those of Heidegger.

[10] The foundation's website is located at http://www.ortegaygasset.edu/fog/ver/61/historia-y-fines/the-foundation-and-its-aims. The page for the *Revista de Occidente* is located at http://www.ortegaygasset.edu/fog/ver/52/revista-de-occidente. You will also find a link at the foundation's website to other publications, including a journal dedicated to Ortega studies. If you are ever in Madrid, feel free to visit the gracious staff at the foundation located at 53 Calle Fortuny in Madrid; I can testify to their hospitality to unannounced visitors when I visited, with children in tow, on May 23, 2011.

[11] The prize is sponsored by the leading Spanish newspaper *El País* (see http://www.prisa.com/en/responsabilidad-social/periodismo-haciendo-escuela/).

[12] Ortega, *QEF*, ed. Garagorri, p. 13; at pp. 17-18 in Mildred Adams' English translation *What Is Philosophy?*, published by W.W. Norton in 1964.

[13] *QEF* at p. 24 (English trans. at p. 30).

[14] See, for example, the statement of Julián Marías that "[w]e Madrid students were then present at the spellbinding and almost unreal spectacle of a philosophy that was *being shaped* before our eyes." Marías, *History*, in "Preface to the English Edition," p. viii (original emphasis). See also the statement of another student of Ortega and another philosopher in his own right, Antonio Rodríguez Huéscar: "In Ortega—in his teaching—we were then in the presence of *living* reason on the march, personalized, unfolding itself; Ortega did not *have* a philosophy, but rather he *was* a philosophy." Antonio Rodríguez Huéscar, *Semblanza de Ortega*, ed. José Lasaga (Barcelona: Editorial Anthropos, 1994), p. 52 (original emphasis; my translation from the Spanish). Are not these accounts the portrayal of a master teacher? Many teach, but few are born to teach by passionately living out what they teach in the lecture hall.

[15] Marías, *Circumstance*, p. 230 (quoting María de Maeztu recalling a class in the College of Education in 1909).

[16] As quoted in Marías, *History*, p. 443.

[17] *QEF*, pp. 61-63 (English trans. at 76-78). Notice that I will also henceforth provide, in a concise form, the parallel page numbers to the English translation of *QEF* by Mildred Adams published by W.W. Norton in 1964 and mentioned above at footnote 3. I choose to capitalize the term "Idealism" to make clear to the general reader that I am referring to a very specific philosophical school and am not using the word in its ordinary sense.

[18] *QEF*, p. 129 (English trans. at 152). As noted earlier, the excerpts from *QEF* ("What is Philosophy?") are my own translations from the original Spanish text edited by Garagorri.

[19] Ortega liked the metaphor of philosophy as sport: "Let us remain, then, at a golden mean, when we theorize and deal with ideas, between the overwhelming seriousness of life, of living, and the irresponsible levity of play. That golden mean is *sport*, which takes from *living* its rigorous effort and takes from play the whim with which it starts." Ortega, *Sobre la razón histórica* (Madrid: Revista de Occidente en Alianza Editorial, 1979), at p. 26 (English title: *On Historical Reason*; original italics; my translation).

[20] *QEF*, p. 129 (English trans. at 153).

[21] Here I must give credit for this terminology ("ancient world view") to Dr. Sandra Rosenthal, a specialist in American pragmatic philosophy, who outlined the history of philosophy to her undergraduate students (which included me) at Loyola University, New Orleans, by describing three world views: the ancient world view, the modern world view (from Descartes to Idealism), and the contemporary world view which would include Ortega y Gasset. Ortega, decades earlier, basically gives this same analysis of the history of philosophy to his own students and listeners.

In an unpublished undergraduate paper from 1983 recognized by The Center for Dewey Studies at Southern Illinois University Carbondale, I made use of Prof. Rosenthal's description of how the contemporary world view of American philosopher John Dewey in particular was a reaction to the ancient and modern world views of previous philosophers:

"With Plato the view that knowledge is about the unchanging and about what is ultimately real culminated in the Divided Line in which true knowledge comes from the contemplation of the Forms.... With the rise of Newtonian science, the Greek-Medieval view that ultimate reality consisted of qualitative forms was challenged by the scientific view, reminiscent of the Atomist school, that the unchanging substances that were ultimately real were not qualitative but *rather quantitative...* . [A] problem arose—the alienation of man from nature. As long as nature was seen as a degenerate reflection of real qualitative Forms, nature could still be seen as qualitative, although inferior. But with the rise of modern science, a metaphysical dualism between the realm of mind and values and the realm of nature and extension resulted. *The split between thought and activity [, seen even among the Greeks, now] led to the split between man and environment.* The Rationalism of Descartes sought the reconciliation of these two realms in the person of an undeceiving God. But the empiricist reaction to rationalism culminated in Humeian skepticism that appropriated and expanded in a serious manner Descartes' project of doubting. The result was disastrous: the doctrine of separation of thought and activity [already evident in the ancient world view of the Greeks] in combination with the results of the new science [of Newton] led to the loss of the very values and qualities for whose preservation the philosophic tradition had, for the most part, been concerned to advance. The Kantian [Idealist] effort to introduce the Non-Spectator Theory of Knowledge to save the certainty destroyed by Hume resulted in an unstable synthesis of the rationalist and empiricist positions. *With the collapse of the absoluteness of Newtonian physics, the Kantian project also collapsed—modern science was not absolute and the unchanging categories suddenly became subject to a scientific revolution. Needless to say, the time had come for a reevaluation of the shattered epistemic tradition of the West and of its social consequences."*

Oswald Sobrino, "The Relevance of John Dewey's Social Philosophy," March 1983, Unpublished paper, pp. 3, 4, and 5 (for those interested, this paper was awarded first place in the John Dewey Undergraduate Essay Contest sponsored by The Center for Dewey Studies in 1983; italics added).

    Note: The technical term "Non-Spectator Theory of Knowledge" refers to the theory of knowledge in which the knower himself is somehow involved with the object of knowledge, in contrast to the "Spectator Theory of Knowledge" in which the knower simply views the object of knowledge as if he or she is a mere uninvolved spectator. Ortega's perspectival theory of knowledge is one example of a Non-Spectator Theory of Knowledge, as is the earlier epistemology of Kant with its human categories that make knowledge possible.

    Both Ortega and Dewey, as exponents of the contemporary world view in philosophy, took upon themselves the task of going beyond the shattered Kantian or Idealist project by proposing a new theory of knowledge and by revising the traditional Western conception of being. Of course, other contemporary philosophers such as Heidegger also pursued this task.

[22] *QEF*, pp. 141-42 (English trans. at 166-67).
[23] Id.
[24] Id. at p. 143 (English trans. at 168).
[25] Id. at p. 128 (English trans. at 152).
[26] Id. at pp. 166-68 (English trans. at 195-98).
[27] Yet, we have to be careful to be a bit nuanced in our characterization of the system itself of Descartes, as noted by the late Fr. Copleston, S.J.: "Descartes certainly tried to ground his philosophy in 'subjectivity' if one means by this that he tried to found his system on the *Cogito, ergo sum*. And it is perfectly true that this was an innovation of importance, and that when one looks back from a later stage of philosophical

development one can see connections between this innovation and later idealism. But though there is what may be called idealist elements in Cartesianism, it would be most misleading to describe the latter as an idealist system." Frederick Copleston, S.J., *A History of Philosophy, Volume IV: From Descartes to Leibniz* (New York: Image Books, 1994), p. 151. My other favorite historian of philosophy, Julián Marías, seems to agree with Fr. Copleston's caution: "Leibniz [1646-1716] is perhaps the first idealist in the strict sense of the word; in Descartes [1596-1650] idealism is still weighed down with realism and Scholastic ideas . . . ." Marías, *History*, p. 238.

[28] Marías, *History*, pp. 222-223 (original italics).

[29] Andrew Dobson, *An Introduction to the Politics and Philosophy of José Ortega y Gasset*, Cambridge Iberian and Latin American Studies (Cambridge University Press, 1989), pp. 128-29. I highly recommend Dobson's book (see my customer review at Amazon.com). For Ortega's use of the term "realism," see *QEF*, pp. 151-52 (English trans. at 177-78).

[30] David Brooks, *The Social Animal: The Hidden Sources of Love, Character, and Achievement* (New York: Random House, 2011).

[31] Brooks, Kindle Locations 3974-4006.

[32] Marías notes the pivotal role of rationalism in the formulation of Descartes' Idealism: "Descartes bases his speculation on . . . . the clearness and distinctness of ideas; it is the self-evidence of reason. Therefore, Descartes' method is rationalism." Marías, *History*, p. 222.

[33] *QEF*, p. 91 (English trans. at 111).

[34] Id. at p. 75 (English trans. at 92).

[35] Frederick Copleston, S.J., "Ortega y Gasset and Philosophical Relativism," *Philosophers and Philosophies* (New York: Barnes & Noble Books, 1976), p. 183.

[36] Julián Marías is my source for two Catholic tidbits about the Jesuit-educated Descartes. First, he notes how Descartes, upon the discovery of his method of doubt "went to Loretto in order to fulfill a vow of gratitude to the Virgin for this discovery" and, second, how Descartes influenced the conversion to Catholicism of the Protestant queen of Sweden. Marías, *History*, p. 212. In addition, another philosopher points out how Descartes viewed his philosophical project as carrying out the vision of a particular Church council, the Fifth Lateran Council (see an abstract of the research of Prof. Aderemi Artis of the University of Michigan-Flint, "Descartes, Luther, and the Fifth Lateran Council," *An Anthology of Philosophical Studies*, available at this link:

http://www.umflint.edu/philosophy/faculty_research.htm#artis_journals).
[37] *QEF*, p. 149 (English trans. at 175).
[38] Id.
[39] Marías, *History*, p. 121 (emphasis added).
[40] *QEF*, p. 144 (English trans. at 169).
[41] Id.
[42] I hope to explore further the relation of Ortega's ideas to Christian ideas in the future, in a continuing series of books on the writings of Ortega.
[43] *QEF*, p. 154 (English trans. at 180-81).
[44] Julián Marías, *Circumstance*, p. 73.
[45] *QEF*, p. 155 (English trans. at 181-82). Let me note for the reader that, in these pages of *QEF*, Ortega again exhibits the delights of his metaphorical style of writing by comparing the intellectual task before him to that of a bullfighter risking death by goring. **My commentary on Ortega is certainly no substitute for reading the original in Spanish or in English translation in order to savor his pleasing metaphors and comparisons**. Yes, philosophy can be clear, pleasing, artistic, and also profound in the hands of a master teacher and writer. That is no small achievement for the good of philosophy itself and impels us not to be fatalistically resigned to the supposed inevitability of turgid, obscure, and jargon-filled writing. We *can* do better. Ortega proved it.
[46] *QEF*, p. 156 (English trans. at 183). This quote can be of help to students of the Bible, especially the Gospels, who puzzle over Jesus' teaching in parables as a way to ferret out those who are really interested in and open to the truth.
[47] Id.
[48] Id. (English trans. at 184).
[49] Id. at p. 158 (English trans. at 186). See the excellent, detailed, and recent entry on Ortega in the *Stanford Encyclopedia of Philosophy* (available at http://plato.stanford.edu/entries/gasset/#ExiPheLif), which I quote in part:

> Ortega's notion of "life as a happening" and the insecurity of human life in the face of death, his analysis of the ontological distinction between human life and things, between "being" and "authentic being," are strikingly similar to ideas which had been formulated by Heidegger in 1927. In *What Is Philosophy?* he aligned his philosophical position with that of Heidegger and the "new philosophy" of being, existence, and human life . . . . Ortega was

quite sensitive to implications drawn on the affinities between his work and Heidegger's, which, in part, explains his efforts to trace the originality of his formulations to his *Meditations*. Apart from a general discussion in his *Idea of Principle in Leibnitz and the Evolution of Deductive Theory* and an essay, "Martin Heidegger and Language of the Philosophers," Ortega referred to Heidegger only in passing in a long footnote in his essay, "Goethe from Within" (published in 1932) (*Obras*, 8: 271–84, 296–300; *Universitas* 7, n.9 (1952): 897–903; *Obras*, 4: 403,541; 9: 625–44).

[50] See the quote from the *Stanford Encyclopedia of Philosophy* in the immediately preceding footnote.
[51] *QEF*, p. 160 (English trans. at 188).
[52] *QEF*, p. 160 (original italics; English trans. at 188).
[53] *QEF*, p. 159 (English trans. at 186).
[54] Id. at p. 161 (English trans. at 189).
[55] Id. at p. 162 (English trans. at 190). As a practical aside for daily life (which is, of course, also a preeminent philosophical concern for those of us who view philosophy as the pursuit of wisdom), note here that friendship implies the freedom to disagree, with mutual respect among friends, even in the most essential matters. If that freedom is missing, then we have to question if we are really practicing friendship that allows the other to be true to his conscience, if what we *call* friendship is really a sort of friendship worth having at all.
[56] Id. at 166 (English trans. at 195).
[57] Id. at 167 (English trans. at 197). Ortega uses Schopenhauer to illustrate this basic equivocation or confused use of "representation," a usage which ignores its double or twofold meaning: the act of representing and what is represented.
[58] Id. at 169 (English trans. at 198). The Spanish phrase is "inseparables, inmediatos y juntos." Ortega makes clear that this advance in philosophical thought is not some puerile or flippant rejection of the great Greek legacy, but rather a conserving of its best insight, namely, that the world is really another and not merely my projection. See *QEF*, p. 171 (English trans. at 201).
[59] Id. at 169 (English trans. at 199).
[60] This dictum appeared in his first book *Meditations on Quixote* published in 1914.
[61] *QEF*, at 170 (emphasis added; English trans. at 200).
[62] Id. at 171 (English trans. at 201).
[63] Id. at 171 (English trans. at 202).

[64] Id. at 173 (English trans. at 203).

[65] Ortega, *Meditaciones del Quijote* (Madrid: Revista de Occidente, 1957; originally published 1914), pp. 43-45 passim. The quoted English translation is by me. I am not sure what Bible verse Ortega is referring to in the quoted excerpt. My guess is that it may be Genesis 32:9, from the Clementine Vulgate: "dixitque Iacob Deus patris mei Abraham et Deus patris mei Isaac Domine qui dixisti mihi revertere in terram tuam et **in locum nativitatis tuae et benefaciam tibi**" (emphasis added). So, maybe, the sense of what Ortega quotes should possibly be more like the following, based on the above portion in bold print: "I will do good for you in the place of your birth," a sense that is also consistent with Ortega's point. [The quoted passage from *Meditaciones del Quijote* can be found at pp. 45-46 of the English translation by Evelyn Rugg and Diego Marín published as *Meditations on Quixote* (New York: W.W. Norton, 1963), with introduction and notes by Julián Marías)].

[66] *QEF*, p. 179 (English trans. at 209-210).

[67] Id. at pp. 179-180 (English trans. at 211).

[68] Id. at 180 (English trans. at 212).

[69] Id. at p. 183 (English trans. at 215).

[70] Id. at p. 184-185 (English trans. at 216-217).

[71] Id. at p. 186 (English trans. at 219).

[72] Id. at p. 187 (English trans. at 219).

[73] Id. at 187 (English trans. at 220).

[74] Id. at pp. 187-88 (English trans. at 220).

[75] Id. at p. 188 (English trans. at 221).

[76] Id. at p. 189 (English trans. at 221).

[77] Id. at p. 211 (English trans. at 248).

[78] Id. at p. 190 (English trans. at 223).

[79] Id. at p. 191 (English trans. at 225).

[80] Marías, *Circumstance*, p. 251. "*[I]t is a pity to carry it [the knowledge of life] unspoken to the grave*; it is a pity not to leave it for others, and 'said' forever. After all, it is the knowledge of what was closest to us; it is our wisdom applied to concrete life, *vital science par excellence*. Year after year we have been amassing this booty, into which we skimmed the riches of our passing life. We wrote books on one subject or another, on the stars or on the Aztecs. And yet we silenced this gift of knowledge which life had made to us as we lived it. I find that it is ungenerous not to return that life to life. Thus, I feel that *every man capable of meditation ought to add to his professional books another book that would communicate his vital knowledge*." *Circumstance*, pp. 250-52 (quoting Ortega writing on or about 1925 in *El Espectador* VII.II, 625;

emphasis added by the author Julián Marías).

[81] *QEF*, at 211 (English trans. at 248); see related footnote 77.

[82] See http://www.focolare.org/en/news/2010/10/23/primo-vescovo-vietnamita-verso-la-santita-2/# (accessed Dec. 20, 2011).

[83] This discussion can be found at *QEF*, pp. 202-203 (English trans. at 237-238).

[84] *QEF*, at p. 203 (English trans. at 238-239).

[85] Id. at p. 204 (English trans. at 239-240; this translation uses "de-living" for my "unliving" at p. 240).

[86] Id. at p. 204 (English trans. at 240).

[87] Julián Marías documents Ortega's pioneering role in the philosophical use of this Greek term in the twentieth century at *Circumstance*, pp. 435, 440-441. Marías discusses in detail the etymology of this term and its apparently later philosophical use by Heidegger at *Circumstance*, pp. 435-444.

[88] Id. at pp. 210-11 (italics added; English trans. at 246-247).

[89] Id. at 211 (English trans. at 248).

Made in the USA
Charleston, SC
21 January 2012